If You Lived When Women Won Their Rights

BY ANNE KAMMA

ILLUSTRATED BY PAMELA JOHNSON

SCHOLASTIC INC.

New York Toronto London Auckland Sydney
Mexico City New Delhi Hong Kong Buenos Aires

Photo credits:
Bettman/CORBIS: pgs 21, 38, 57;
Coline Jenkins/Elizabeth Cady Stanton Trust: p. 26.
Library of Congress: p. 29.
The cartoon on page 54 is from the Library of Congress (LC-USZ62-51821).

ISBN-13: 978-0-439-74869-8
ISBN-10: 0-439-74869-0

Text copyright © 2006 by Anne Kamma
Illustrations copyright © 2006 by Pamela Johnson

25   24   23   22   21   17 18/0

Printed in the U.S.A.   40
This edition first printing, February 2008

Cover design by David Neuhaus

For Ellen

ACKNOWLEDGMENTS

With grateful thanks to the many helpful people at the Women's Rights National Historical Park, Seneca Falls, NY, including: Anne Derousie, historian; Tina Orcutt, superintendent; David Malone; Jason Boyd and Jack Shay, park rangers. Thanks also to Jeffrey Flannery, manuscript librarian, Manuscript Reading Room, Library of Congress, Washington, D.C.; Kay Crank, Battenkill Books, Cambridge, NY; Susan Gordis, MJFA; Lise Kreps; Ellen Levine, for her insightful review of my manuscript; Pene McCain; Toby Yuen; and my wonderful editor, Eva Moore.

CONTENTS

Introduction

How would you feel if someone said you weren't allowed to
- ride a bike?
- play most sports?
- go to college?

And when you grew up, how would you feel if you weren't allowed to
- speak in front of an audience with men in it?
- vote?
- be a doctor, lawyer, scientist, or politician?

If you lived in the 1800s, that's how it was for girls and women. Girls were supposed to stay home, like their mothers. They learned to cook and sew and take care of the house. They were supposed to be quiet and obey their elders.

Girls were told they weren't as smart as boys. When they grew up and got married, the law said they had to obey their husbands.

But many women in the 1800s didn't think this was fair. That's why, in 1848, they joined together to fight for their rights as human beings.

This book tells you what happened.

HISTORY TIME LINE
This book is mostly about the years shown in the colored part of this time line.

1620	1775–1783	1788	1848	1861–1865	1868/1870	1893	1914–1918	1920
The Pilgrims land at Plymouth Rock.	The 13 American colonies fight for independence from England in the American Revolution.	The United States Constitution becomes the law of the land. Only white men may vote.	The Women's Rights Movement begins in Seneca Falls, New York.	The Civil War is fought. Slaves are set free.	African-American men are given the right to vote.	New Zealand is the first nation in the world to give women the right to vote.	World War I	American women win the right to vote.

Under 1775–1783:

1776

The Declaration of Independence is signed.

Under 1914–1918:

1917

America enters the war.

What rights did the first women who settled in America have?

When the Pilgrims came to America, they brought their English laws with them. And in England, women didn't have many rights.

After the *Mayflower* landed, only men were allowed to vote on what kind of government the new colony should have. The Pilgrims' religion also taught that men should rule over women.

Yet there were women in this New World who were treated fairly. Among the Iroquois Indians, who often lived near the English settlers, men and women were equal. The women farmed and owned the land. Men were the hunters, warriors, and chiefs. But women picked the chiefs. If a chief didn't do a good job, the women picked another chief instead.

Did women help win the American Revolution?

Yes. Women kept the farms and businesses going while the men were away at war. Some even helped in the fight for independence from England.

The day after the British defeated the Americans at Lexington and Concord, women in a nearby town defended a bridge against the retreating British. The women grabbed muskets and pitchforks and captured a group of enemy soldiers.

Some women carried water to cool down cannons on the battlefield. The soldiers called them "Molly Pitchers." Mary Hays made the name Molly Pitcher famous. When her husband fell in battle, she took his place at the cannon and kept on firing.

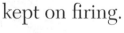

Deborah Sampson pretended to be a man and joined the army. She fought in many raids and was wounded in battle. After the war, she received an army pension.

Women like Deborah and Mary became heroes during the Revolution.

Thousands of women worked in the American army. They nursed the wounded soldiers, washed their laundry, and carried heavy burdens from camp to camp. Other women were spies. Deborah Champion was only twenty-two years old when she rode for two days through enemy territory to bring secret military information to General George Washington.

Why did Abigail Adams write to her husband?

Women had helped win the war. And it was written in the Declaration of Independence that "all men are created equal." But did that mean women, too? Abigail Adams wanted to make sure it did. So she wrote a letter to her husband, John Adams, who was helping to write America's new laws.

English law said that husbands were the masters, and their wives had to obey them. Abigail wanted husbands and wives to be friends and equals. "Don't put such unlimited power into the hands of the husbands," Abigail wrote. People become tyrants if they have too much power. It is human nature, she said.

Abigail also wanted women to have a voice in America's new government. People shouldn't have to obey laws they had no part in making. Wasn't that what the Declaration of Independence said?

John Adams was a very important man. He later became the president of the United States. What did he think about his wife's ideas? "I cannot but laugh," he wrote to Abigail. John Adams thought it was silly to think that women were equal to men. He also didn't think that Native Americans and African Americans were equal to white people. In those days, it was only white men who were "created equal."

Did laws about women change after the American Revolution?

No. Our founding fathers took English laws, called common law, and made them part of American laws. Husbands still ruled over their wives.

Women even lost some rights. Before the Revolution, a few states, such as New Jersey, allowed women to vote if they owned property. After independence was won, that right was taken away.

Which laws upset women the most?

The marriage laws.

How were the laws unfair to married women?

When a woman married, she lost everything she owned— her money, her land, her personal things. By law, everything now belonged to her husband. She didn't even own the dresses she wore, or the presents she got for her birthday.

Today, if your parents get divorced, both your mother and your father usually have the right to keep seeing you. But that's not how it used to be. In the 1800s, children belonged to the father. It didn't matter if he was a good parent or a bad one. Mothers had no right to keep their children, not even little babies.

So, if your parents got divorced back then, you would probably live with your father, unless he said you could stay with your mother. But he could also send you away to live with someone else. If he was angry with your mother, he could stop her from ever seeing you until you grew up.

What did girls wear?

Girls always wore dresses — never pants.

You could tell a girl's age by the length of her dress. If it was just below the knees, she was twelve or younger. By the time she was fourteen, the dress was halfway to her ankles. At sixteen, it was at her ankles. At eighteen, a girl's dress reached the floor, just like her mother's.

Girls' clothes weren't made for running and playing the way they are today. Skirts had to look full, so girls wore petticoats — sometimes as many as ten. Often they were stiff and heavy.

In the 1850s, someone invented a new, light petticoat. It had wire hoops and looked like a birdcage. Girls liked it better because it was easier to move their legs underneath it. Still, the hoops got in your way when you played. And when the wind blew, you had to hang on to your skirt.

Why did women complain about their clothes?

Women's clothes were heavy. A skirt and petticoats might weigh as much as fifteen pounds! Some women wore hip pads to help carry the weight.

Long skirts dragged in the dirt and mud. Remember, in those days, most streets weren't paved as they are today. And it was easy to trip on your skirt and petticoats when you walked upstairs.

The corsets were worst of all. Women were supposed to have tiny waists. Otherwise, people didn't think they looked pretty. The tighter the laces on a corset were pulled, the smaller your waist became. Even young girls sometimes wore corsets.

Corsets were made with whalebone or steel to make them stiff. You could hardly bend over. Corsets squeezed your ribs and lungs so tightly you couldn't breathe normally. That's why women sometimes fainted when they danced or exercised. Men thought that fainting showed how weak and delicate women were. But it really showed that their corsets were too tight.

What a lady wore in 1860

1. First came the undershirt and long cotton underpants.
2. Then came the corset.
3. Next, a lady had to step into the "cage" and tie it to her waist.
4. Then, she put on the petticoats.
5. Then, finally, came the dress.

Did girls go to school?

Most girls did not go to school before the American Revolution. But that changed after the Revolution. People thought girls should go to school so that later they could teach their sons how to be good citizens in America's new democracy.

In the 1800s, boys and girls went to elementary school together. School was often free because America was building more and more public schools. But very few girls went to high school. Those who did were lucky. Once they had a high school education they could work as teachers.

Why weren't women allowed to go to college?

"Women's brains are too small." "They're not as smart as men." "They can't learn science or mathematics."

That's what the male experts said.

Emma Willard knew the men were wrong. As a girl, she loved mathematics, and she wished that women could go to college to study it. But there were no colleges that accepted women. So, in 1821, Emma started the Troy Female Seminary in Troy, New York. The school taught subjects more like those taught in college.

Emma got in trouble because of her new ideas. One day, visitors walked into a classroom while a student was drawing a picture of the heart and circulatory system on the blackboard. The visitors were shocked. Women were not supposed to see pictures of the human body. The pictures might upset their delicate nature.

Then, in 1833, something wonderful happened. A college that accepted women students finally opened. It was Oberlin College in Ohio. Soon women were taking the same classes as men and earning college degrees.

But Oberlin also wanted its female students to remember their role as women. So female students had to wash male students' clothes, clean their rooms, and serve them at mealtimes.

Who was Lucy Stone?

"Is the child crazy?" That's what Lucy Stone's father said when he heard she wanted to go to college as her older brothers had. But Lucy went to college anyway, even though she had to pay for it herself.

Lucy was a rebel in other ways as well. She didn't believe God wanted men to rule over women, as her parents and church told her.

She was a rebel at Oberlin College, too. When she made a speech to help celebrate the end of slavery in the West Indies, the college was very upset. Women didn't speak in public! Wasn't Lucy frightened and embarrassed to speak on the same stage with men?

She even caused trouble at her graduation. Lucy refused to write her graduation essay unless she was allowed to read it at the ceremony, just as the men students were. Why should a man read *her* essay aloud? Other students supported her, but the college said no.

After college, an antislavery group hired Lucy. She traveled the country speaking out against slavery and the unfair treatment of women. Her family was horrified, but Lucy was a great success. Her beautiful, bell-like voice and quiet ways could make even the worst heckler stop and listen.

How did women earn money?

It wasn't easy. The few jobs women could get — such as sewing, factory work, and teaching — paid very little. When Susan B. Anthony was a schoolteacher, the men teachers in her school earned $10 a week. Susan was one of the best teachers. But because she was a woman, she earned $2.50. Like Susan, most women didn't earn very much money in those days.

Some women got rich when they went out West. Clara Brown, an ex-slave, made so much money cooking and washing for Colorado gold miners that she ended up owning part of a gold mine. She used some of her money to buy covered wagons to bring thirty-four of her Kentucky relatives to Colorado.

A few women got rich inventing things. Margaret Knight invented a machine that made brown paper bags with square bottoms — just like the ones we use today.

What was America like in the 1800s?

Big changes were happening. Machines were invented that produced things faster and cheaper. Families left their farms and moved to towns and cities to work in factories.

The 1800s was also a time when people had lots of new ideas about how to make the United States a better place. Some groups wanted to end slavery. They were called abolitionists. Other groups wanted to improve hospitals. The biggest group of all wanted to make it against the law to drink alcohol.

Why did people want to make alcohol illegal?

By the 1800s, alcohol was a big problem in America. If there was a get-together, chances are you'd find men drinking heavily. Some store owners gave a man a drink of whiskey if he bought something. There were bars everywhere.

Many workers got whiskey as part of their pay, and they took "rum breaks" the way we take coffee breaks today.

The problem was so bad, some people got together to ban alcohol. They started the temperance movement.

Women had special reasons for joining the temperance movement. When husbands spent their wages on whiskey, families were left with no money for food and rent. Men could even take the money their wives and children earned and spend it on drinking — the law gave them the right. Drunken husbands were also more likely to hurt their wives and children.

Many women joined temperance groups. They felt that it was the only way to protect their homes.

Did women join the antislavery movement?

Yes. Women were a big part of the antislavery movement. Among the most famous were the Grimké sisters.

Sarah and Angelina Grimké were daughters of a wealthy South Carolina slave owner. As girls, they hated slavery. When they grew up, they went north and joined the abolitionists. At first, they spoke only to women in private homes.

But so many women wanted to hear about slavery that Sarah and Angelina did something brave. They became the first women abolitionists to speak in public auditoriums.

They were so popular, even men began to come to hear their lectures.

Most people were shocked to learn that women had spoken in front of men. Newspapers called Sarah and Angelina "unnatural." Church leaders said that women should be silent and let men do the talking. They warned that independent women who "acted like men" would end up shamed and dishonored.

But Sarah and Angelina kept on speaking. Soon other women abolitionists started speaking in public, too.

Who was Elizabeth Cady Stanton?

Elizabeth Cady Stanton was born in a small town in upstate New York. When she was a little girl, she would listen in her father's law office as married women begged for help. Sometimes they and their children were left homeless because their husbands had spent all their wages on whiskey. Sometimes a husband had sold the house a wife had inherited from her parents.

Elizabeth's father always told the women there was nothing he could do to help. The law was the law.

Little Elizabeth was so upset she decided to take her scissors and cut the bad laws out of her father's law books. Her father had to explain to her that only the lawmakers in the government could "cut out" bad laws. Maybe when she grew up, he said, she could ask them to do that.

As Elizabeth grew older, she noticed other ways that girls and women were treated unfairly. Girls were told they weren't as smart and important as boys. And when Elizabeth wanted to go to college, just as her brother had, no college in America took women students. That wasn't fair, she thought.

What started the women's rights movement?

When Elizabeth Cady Stanton married, she and her husband, Henry, went to London so Henry could go to the World Antislavery Convention.

On the first day, a fight broke out over whether women should be allowed to take part in the convention. Women shouldn't go to public meetings, some argued. They should stay at home where they belong! Ministers waved their Bibles and said that God had made woman to obey man. Some yelled, "Turn the women out!"

The women were not allowed to speak. When the vote was taken, most of the men voted to keep women out. They were taken to a segregated section where they could watch, but not speak.

The women were furious about the way they had been treated. Elizabeth Cady Stanton and Lucretia Mott decided to do something about it when they returned home to America.

What did the women do?

In the summer of 1848, Lucretia Mott came to Seneca Falls, New York, where Elizabeth Cady Stanton lived. Now, Elizabeth thought, was the time to have a women's rights convention — the first one ever.

Together with three other women, Elizabeth and Lucretia planned the convention for the following Wednesday, July nineteenth. The rush was on! They put an ad in the local paper and sat down to plan the meeting. They knew they had to explain what women wanted. But how should they write it? Elizabeth had the answer — write it like the Declaration of Independence. After all, weren't women declaring their independence? Weren't "all men *and women* created equal"?

They also wrote a list of important ideas they wanted the people at the convention to vote on.

Now they were ready.

Who was Lucretia Mott?

Lucretia Mott grew up on Nantucket Island—a place very different from most places in America in the 1800s. Her father was the captain of a whaleboat. Because the men were at sea, fishing and hunting whales for months at a time, women ran the island businesses. Lucretia grew up seeing strong women who knew how to do "men's work" and talk to men as equals.

Lucretia and her family were Quakers. The Quakers believed that Christ's inner light lived in everyone, and that all people were equal before God. When Lucretia was a girl, the Quakers belonged to the only church in the country to allow women ministers.

Quakers believed in educating girls, so Lucretia's father sent her to a Quaker academy. She continued reading and studying after she married and had children. In time, Lucretia became a Quaker minister and a leader in the abolitionist and women's rights movements. She also worked for justice for Native Amercans and many other causes. She was respected by everyone, even those who disagreed with her.

Did anybody show up?

Lucretia Mott was worried. It was the haying season, so the farmers were busy. And the ad had been in the newspaper for only a week. Would anybody show up?

On the morning of the convention, there were just a few carts on the road at first. But soon vehicles of all kinds appeared — horse-drawn carriages, fancy pony carts, farm wagons — all heading toward Seneca Falls. By the time they reached town, the roads were jammed.

Nineteen-year-old Charlotte Woodward came with her friends. She worked in her bedroom sewing for a glove factory because women weren't supposed to work outside the home. When she was paid, her father kept the money. She didn't think that was fair at all. "Every fiber of my being rebelled," she remembered.

A huge crowd — mostly women — gathered outside the Wesleyan Chapel, where the convention was to be held. When the doors opened, people rushed in and filled every seat.

What happened at the Seneca Falls Convention?

There must have been a lot of excitement in the audience. This was the first women's rights convention ever held anywhere in the world. And women were going to speak to an audience with men in it!

Everything went well the first day. First, Lucretia Mott explained to the audience why a women's movement was necessary. Then Elizabeth Cady Stanton read the Declaration of Sentiments, which was a list of the wrongs done by men to women in 1848:

- Women have no voice in their government.
- Colleges are closed to women.
- Women have no right to their children.
- Women's husbands take their property and wages.
- Men keep all the high-paying jobs for themselves.

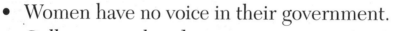

Elizabeth was nervous. This was the first time she had ever spoken in front of an audience. As she read, however, her voice became stronger and stronger. But would the audience vote to approve the Declaration of Sentiments?

The convention organizers held their breath. "Yes!" came the answer. Afterward, many of the people in the audience signed their names to the Declaration of Sentiments.

Was there trouble at the convention?

The next day, Elizabeth read the list of important ideas and asked the audience to vote on them:

Did everyone agree that men and women were created equal? Yes!

Did they agree that women should be allowed to speak in public? Yes!

Did they agree that women should be allowed to speak out in church? Yes!

As Elizabeth went down the list, the audience agreed with everything except one question: Did everyone agree that women should have the right to vote?

Even Lucretia Mott worried that asking for the vote might make the convention look silly. Elizabeth's husband had already left town so people wouldn't think he agreed with such a ridiculous idea.

An argument broke out. Angry words were spoken. But Elizabeth refused to back down. "The right is ours," she said. "Have it we must. Use it we will."

Just when it looked as if the audience might vote "no," Frederick Douglass rose to speak. Everybody knew who he was — the great abolitionist leader who had been a slave. Without the vote, he argued, there is no freedom. That is true for black and white, men and women.

In the end, most of the audience voted "yes."

What did the newspapers say?

Most newspapers had only bad things to say about the Seneca Falls Convention. They called the leaders "monsters." Wanting equal rights with men, the papers said, was dangerous and ridiculous. Women belonged in the home. "A woman is nobody. A wife is everything," one Philadelphia newspaper reporter wrote.

And it wasn't just the newspapers. Ministers and neighbors — even friends — attacked the convention. Only a few newspapers, such as the *New-York Tribune* and the abolitionist papers, supported the women.

Were the people from the convention upset?

They were very upset. Nobody had expected such an attack. Some were so embarrassed they had their names removed from the Declaration of Sentiments. Elizabeth Cady Stanton's own sister, Harriet Eaton, was forced by her husband to remove her name.

Others refused to go to any more women's meetings. They were afraid of seeing their names in the newspapers.

Most of the women still believed in women's rights. But many felt like the wife of Senator William Seward: "I'm with you thoroughly, but I'm a born coward. There is nothing I dread more than Mr. Seward's ridicule."

Was the convention a failure?

Elizabeth Cady Stanton didn't think so. After all, the women's movement had finally begun — the first in the world. And the leaders were already planning to have another convention in just two weeks.

Even the terrible newspaper articles helped, Elizabeth thought. Before the convention, almost nobody had talked about women's rights. Now the whole country was talking. You couldn't open a newspaper without reading about it. Some papers had printed the whole Declaration of Sentiments.

"It will start women thinking, and men too," she said, "and that is the first step."

Who was the leader of the new movement?

Elizabeth Cady Stanton. The Seneca Falls Convention made her famous. And to her own surprise, she turned out to be a great speaker.

Something else made her a good leader — she could think on her feet. When people all around her became angry, she stayed cool and always had a good answer.

Elizabeth was also smart. She read books on law, history, philosophy, science, and politics. In fact, if she had been a man, she probably would have become an important judge or senator.

But Elizabeth had a problem. She was a mother with children and a house to take care of. She didn't have time to travel across the country to conventions. That's why it was lucky she met Susan B. Anthony. Susan did have time. She wasn't married, so she could leave home whenever she wanted.

Who was Susan B. Anthony?

Susan B. Anthony grew up in a loving Quaker family. Her aunt Hannah was a Quaker minister, and Susan was used to seeing women treated with respect.

But Susan also saw how hard her mother worked. Workers from her father's mill lived in the Anthony home. And there were six children to take care of. Susan and her two sisters helped their mother as soon as they were old enough. But she watched her once-smiling mother become quiet and sad because of the endless work.

Susan loved going to the plain, one-room schoolhouse in Battenville, New York. One day, after studying arithmetic, she asked the teacher to show her how to do long division. When her teacher told her that girls didn't need to learn higher mathematics, Susan's father took her out of school. Then he hired a teacher and started his own school. Unlike most people at the time, Daniel Anthony believed that girls should have as good an education as boys.

Susan was taught to care about fairness and justice. When she grew up, she worked to end slavery. And when she met Elizabeth Cady Stanton, they teamed up to lead the new women's rights movement.

What happened when Susan B. Anthony and Elizabeth Cady Stanton became a team?

Fireworks! They became one of the greatest teams in American history.

Susan B. Anthony was a genius at organizing. She arranged every part of a meeting — rented an auditorium, got the flyers printed, planned the program, raised money, and hired excellent speakers. She was also great at finding new ways to make politicians pay attention.

But Susan was not good at writing speeches and articles. Elizabeth was good at writing. And she was a daring thinker. Her articles were published in newspapers and magazines all over America.

So Susan organized, and Elizabeth stayed home and wrote Susan's speeches, as well as other kinds of writing. Only rarely did Elizabeth go out and make her own speeches. That had to wait until her children were a little older.

Did any men support women's rights?

Many did. Some were abolitionists, like Frederick Douglass, who fought to end slavery. Others were Quakers.

There were also men who simply thought women were being treated unfairly. One man gave $5,000 to the women's movement when he saw how much his married daughter suffered because of unfair marriage laws. Horace Greeley, who owned the *New-York Tribune*, sometimes supported women's rights. He printed articles by Elizabeth Cady Stanton in his newspaper.

But in the 1800s, most men were against women's rights.

Did the marriage laws change?

Yes. In 1860, after years of hard work by the women's movement, some of the laws were changed.

Now a woman could keep the money she earned. She didn't have to give it to her husband. And now she could own things. Her husband wasn't allowed to take them or sell them.

Best of all, children now belonged to both parents — not just the father.

The first state to change the laws was New York, but soon other states followed. It was a big victory for women. For the first time, a married woman wasn't penniless and had equal rights to her children.

Why did it take so long to change the laws?

If you can vote, you have power. Politicians have to listen to you because they need your vote. But women couldn't vote in the 1800s. So when they asked a politician to change the laws, he didn't have to pay attention.

So, how did women get men to change the laws? By making speeches, writing articles, and holding women's rights conventions. Little by little, more and more people agreed that women should have equal rights.

Women also got thousands of people to sign petitions asking the government to change the laws. And when the lawmakers refused to act, the women came back the next year with more petitions.

Finally, after many years, the laws were changed.

What happened when women first wore pants?

Amelia Bloomer was amazed when she saw what Elizabeth Cady Stanton and her cousin Elizabeth Smith Miller were wearing. Pants!

Amelia immediately sewed herself a pair. No women had dared to wear pants before.

When Amelia wrote about her new pants in her newspaper, *The Lily*, hundreds of women sent letters asking for information about how to make them. Amelia printed the sewing instructions, and soon women all over America were wearing the new pants. Amelia Bloomer became so famous that the pants were called bloomers.

Women working on farms and in factories — even women pioneers on the Oregon Trail — liked the freedom of bloomers. But women didn't like the jeering boys and men who followed them in the streets, sometimes throwing eggs and stones at them. Newspapers made fun of "bloomer girls." And ministers told women that wearing pants was against God's will.

"Wearing the pants" means being the one who runs things. In those days, most men thought they, not women, should run things. Cartoons made fun of husbands whose wives wore pants.

Women's friends and family also didn't like the new fashion. Elizabeth Cady Stanton's sister burst into tears when she heard Elizabeth was wearing bloomers. Elizabeth's sons begged her not to visit them in school. Lucy Stone and Susan B. Anthony were trapped by a mob of taunting men on a New York City street and had to be rescued.

The teasing got so bad that, in the end, women gave up wearing the comfortable pants. But that wasn't the end of the bloomer story. Thirty years later, the bloomer craze came back. It was all because of the invention of the bicycle.

Bloomers were long, baggy pants. They were tied at the ankle, with a ruffle at the bottom, because women in the 1800s never showed their ankles. Women wore short dresses over their bloomers.

When bicycles first came out, only men rode them. Women were told they might hurt themselves if they rode a bicycle. Some men just didn't like the idea of giving women so much freedom. One city even had a law against women riding bicycles on the streets.

That all changed in the 1890s. Women and girls decided to ride bicycles anyway. And the best costume for bicycle riding was — you guessed it — bloomers! This time people didn't laugh and throw things when women wore pants. But women could wear their bloomers only when they went bicycling. Afterwards, they had to go back to their long skirts.

What was different about the West?

Pioneer women were respected for their hard work. Men knew that without their wives, their homesteads might fail. So they treated women more like equals. And there were very few women in the West, so men were really glad when a woman settled nearby.

Women did new things in the West. They ran their own ranches and farms. Some became cowgirls, sheriffs, mayors, and judges. Girls were free to do more, too. Eunice Norris, an African-American cowgirl, helped her family build their log cabin in Colorado.

Agnes Cleaveland became a great rider, even though she had to ride sidesaddle, as girls did in those days. One newspaper declared that Agnes and a man named Three-fingered Pete were the "best riders in the country."

How did pioneers in the West find out about the women's movement?

In the 1800s there was no television or radio. Women leaders such as Elizabeth Cady Stanton traveled all over the West giving speeches about women's rights.

The pioneers loved it when speakers came to their little towns. That's how they learned about the outside world. The speaker might be a general, an actor, or someone with radical new ideas. To the pioneers it was all great fun.

But it wasn't easy for speakers to get to those small towns. When it rained, the unpaved roads turned into mud. Then it was hard for the stagecoaches to get through. And rivers froze, sometimes trapping boats in ice for hours.

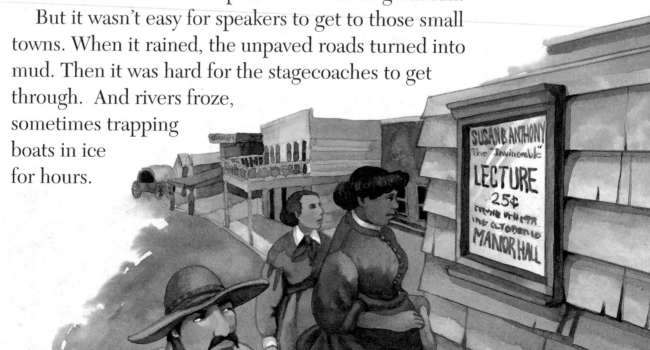

SUSAN B ANTHONY
The "Invincible"
LECTURE
25¢
MANOR HALL

When big snowstorms hit, the trains stopped running. That's what happened once to Elizabeth Cady Stanton's train. But she had to be in the next town that evening to give a speech, so she hired a horse-drawn sled. Bundled up in a fur coat with a thick scarf over her head and face, and a heated wooden board under her feet, she was ready.

The driver threw a large buffalo robe over her and tied the two buffalo tails around her neck. "If you sit perfectly still, you'll come out all right," he said.

In spite of huge snowdrifts and freezing winds, the sled made it across the prairie in six hours — just in time for Elizabeth's eight o'clock speech.

How did women get the vote in Wyoming?

Before Esther Morris moved to Wyoming, she lived in the East, where she had heard Susan B. Anthony speak. In 1869, Esther invited some politicians over for tea at her home in South Pass City. She wanted to talk to them about giving Wyoming women the vote.

Those against women voting said that men were often drunk and rowdy at the polls. Women were too delicate, they said, to vote in such a rough, male world. Besides, women weren't smart enough.

But Esther disagreed. If you give Wyoming women the vote, she said, more women will want to come here and settle. And Wyoming needs more settlers. We have too many rowdy miners, cowboys, railroad workers, and gamblers who never stay in one place.

She also said that if women could vote, they would vote for law and order. And Wyoming was a lawless place in 1869.

The politicians agreed. That same year, Wyoming became the first place in America to give women the vote.

Was there trouble when the women voted?

No. Whenever a woman approached the voting place, word would go out: "Psst! Be quiet! A woman is coming!" And the men would respectfully let her pass.

It was the quietest election anyone in Wyoming had ever seen!

What did women do during the Civil War?

During the Civil War, from 1861 to 1865, women stopped working for their own rights.

Because men were away fighting, women on both sides — the North and the South — ran farms and businesses. They worked in "men's jobs" to support their families.

Women also provided most of the food, clothing, and medicine for the two armies. They trained nurses and ran army hospitals.

Clara Barton nursed soldiers on some of the bloodiest battlefields of the war. She didn't care if the wounded men were from the North or the South. They all deserved medical care. After the war, she started the American Red Cross, which still helps people today when disaster strikes.

Before the Civil War began, Harriet Tubman helped hundreds of slaves escape to freedom. During the war, she was a spy and a leader for the Northern army. She was called "General Tubman" because she sometimes took soldiers into battle. She once led three gunboats up the Combahee River, where the soldiers surprised the Southern army and destroyed a railroad and a bridge.

Who was Sojourner Truth?

Sojourner Truth was born a slave in New York State. Her owner wouldn't let her marry the man she loved and forced her to marry someone else. She had thirteen children but saw most of them sold into slavery.

After New York ended slavery in 1827, Sojourner became a preacher. She traveled the country speaking out against slavery and the unequal treatment of women. Her powerful voice and piercing eyes made her one of the most famous speakers of the time.

Once she was at a women's rights meeting in Ohio. Men in the audience were shouting at the women, trying to break up the meeting. Sojourner rose to speak. She answered a man who said that women were too weak and helpless to be allowed to vote:

"That man over there says that women need to be helped into carriages, and lifted over ditches, and have the best place everywhere. Nobody ever helps me into carriages, and over puddles, or gives me the best place. And ain't I a woman?

"Look at me! Look at my arm! I have ploughed, and planted, and gathered into barns, and no man could head me! And ain't I a woman? I could work as much and eat as much as a man — when I could get it — and bear the lash as well! And ain't I a woman?"

When she was finished, the crowd stood up and cheered.

Why were women's rights leaders upset after the war?

After the Civil War, the Constitution was changed to allow African-American men to vote — but not women, black or white.

Susan B. Anthony and Elizabeth Cady Stanton were furious. For sixteen years the women's movement had fought for the right to vote. And they had fought hard to end slavery as well. Finally, there was a chance to change the Constitution so that both women and African Americans could vote. Instead, women were told to wait. Even most antislavery leaders agreed.

Sojourner Truth didn't agree. "There is a great stir about colored men getting their rights," she said, "but not a word about colored women." She warned, "If the colored men get their rights, and not the colored women . . . the colored men will be masters over the women."

Sojourner worried about something else, too. If women didn't get the vote now, it might be a long time before they had another chance.

She was right. It took fifty-three more years. Both Sojourner Truth and Elizabeth Cady Stanton died without ever having a chance to vote.

Susan B. Anthony did vote — once. When she was fifty-three years old, Susan talked a voting inspector into letting her vote in a presidential election. But soon afterward she was arrested for breaking the law. There was a trial. The judge wouldn't even let Susan speak. The judge found her guilty and told her to pay a fine of $100. Susan said she would not pay. And she never did.

Two years later, the Supreme Court, the highest court in the United States, declared that the Constitution did not give women the right to vote. It was up to the states to decide who should vote, the Court said.

When women heard this, they began a long fight to change the Constitution.

The United States Constitution was written in 1787. It tells how the government will work and what rights the people have.

Over the years, changes — called amendments — have been added to the Constitution. An amendment must be approved by three-quarters of the states before it can become a law of the land. The Fourteenth and Fifteenth amendments of 1868 and 1870 gave African-American men the right to vote.

This cartoon makes fun of giving women the right to vote. It shows the wife taking over the husband's "job" of voting while he stays home with the babies. Most men in those days thought this was a silly idea.

How did women speakers help change America?

In the 1870s, most people had never actually heard a woman speak about women's rights. Newspapers called women speakers "female monsters." So imagine how surprised an audience was when Elizabeth Cady Stanton stepped up to speak. By now she was a plump little woman with pretty gray curls who looked like a cheerful grandmother. She was funny when she spoke, and she made a lot of sense. Even those who didn't agree with her often respected her.

For many years, speakers such as Susan B. Anthony and Elizabeth Cady Stanton traveled across the country. Slowly, more and more people began to agree that women should have equal rights. Newspapers and politicians began to show more respect — and to take women's rights more seriously.

By 1900, things were a lot better for women in the United States. But there was one thing most women still didn't have — the right to vote.

How did suffragists in England help?

By 1910, it looked like most American women would never get the vote. Only a few states had given women the vote. New ideas were needed.

Something new was happening in England. Suffragists there had decided they weren't going to wait quietly any longer. Without equality, there would be no peace. They interrupted government speakers, heckled politicians, and held noisy meetings on street corners and in parks. Police and bystanders often attacked them. Many protesters were arrested and put in jail. Some suffragists set mailboxes on fire, cut telephone wires, and threw rocks through government building windows.

In England, nobody could ignore women's suffrage anymore. An American, Alice Paul, had worked with the English suffragists and liked some of their ideas. Now she was coming home to continue the fight.

What is a suffragist?

A suffragist (SUHF-ri-jist) is a person who fights for the right to vote. It comes from the word suffrage, which means having the right to vote.

Who was Alice Paul?

Alice was a Quaker. While studying in England, she joined the suffragists and was arrested many times.

After she came back to the United States, she and her friend Lucy Burns worked together to win the vote here.

Like Martin Luther King, Jr., Alice Paul led nonviolent protests. When picketing the White House, the women stood in dignified silence, no matter how angry the crowd around them got. Alice was admired for being brave, and for never giving up — even when people yelled at her.

Many people thought Carrie Chapman Catt, another women's rights leader, was more respectable, and that Alice was a troublemaker. But it took both Carrie, "the General," and Alice, "the troublemaker," to finally win the vote for women.

Who was Carrie Chapman Catt?

Carrie grew up on an Iowa farm, where she had to ride five miles on horseback to get to school. Nobody imagined that one day she would grow up to be a great women's rights leader.

What Carrie wanted most was for women to get the vote. She became the next Susan B. Anthony, because she was a genius at organizing and planning. She was called "the General" and planned her battles like a military campaign. Together with Alice Paul, she led the final fight that won the vote for women.

Why did Alice Paul organize a march in Washington, D.C.?

Alice Paul wanted Congress to change the Constitution so that all women could vote. That's why she planned a big march in Washington, D.C.— something women had never done before.

As thousands of women from all over the United States marched peacefully down Pennsylvania Avenue, they were attacked by an angry mob of men. Police refused to protect the marchers. Finally, a group of male students in the crowd locked arms and formed a protective chain around some of the women. By the time the U.S. Cavalry arrived to restore order, hundreds had been injured.

Newspapers and the public were shocked at the way the women had been treated. People began to pay more attention to the suffragists, and many more women joined the movement.

What did Alice Paul do next?

On a cold January morning in 1917, twelve women unfurled their banners in front of the White House, where President Woodrow Wilson lived. HOW LONG MUST WOMEN WAIT FOR LIBERTY? read one banner. MR. PRESIDENT, WHAT WILL YOU DO FOR WOMEN'S SUFFRAGE? another stated. Alice's next plan had begun.

Picketing the White House was something new. The women stood on the sidewalk, silently holding their banners. At first nobody bothered them. But things changed when America entered World War I three months later.

President Wilson said America was fighting the war in Europe to "make the world safe for democracy." People, he said, should have a "voice in their own government."

That's what the suffragists thought, too! Soon there were banners in front of the White House asking President Wilson why he supported democracy for people in Europe, but not democracy for American women. The president was embarrassed — and angry. Onlookers attacked the picketers and called them unpatriotic.

Did the police arrest the attackers? No. They arrested the women! Their crime? Blocking traffic. They weren't even guilty; it was the crowds that blocked traffic. But hundreds of women were arrested and sent to jail.

What was the "Night of Terror"?

Each day more and more women were put in jail.

Then, on November 15, 1917, the prison guards decided to teach the women a lesson. In a rage, they hurled one woman into a cell, smashing her head and knocking her out. Her cell mate, who thought she was dead, had a heart attack. Another woman was thrown through the air, hitting the cell wall. Others were shoved, thrown, and knocked down. It became known as the Night of Terror.

In protest, Alice Paul and other women in jail went on a hunger strike. So the prison officials forced them to eat. Guards pushed tubes down the women's throats and poured food down the tubes. It was very painful.

The prison also tried to have Alice, their leader, declared insane so they could send her to a mental institution. Luckily, the psychiatrist brought in to examine her didn't agree. He said she wasn't crazy. She was just brave.

When word got out about how the women were being treated, people were horrified. All the women were released from jail. In spite of their suffering, the suffragists had won a big victory. Now even more people supported them.

When did women get the right to vote?

To change the Constitution, thirty-six states had to vote to approve the amendment.

On August 18, 1920, all eyes were on Tennessee. Thirty-five states had already approved the Nineteenth Amendment to give women the vote. America's women were just one state away from victory. But how would the Tennessee lawmakers vote?

Everyone knew it would be close. One lawmaker was brought from the hospital to cast his vote. Another rushed to vote before going home to his dying child. Just when it looked like the amendment would fail, Harry Burn stood up. In his pocket was a letter from his mother. "Hurrah! And vote for suffrage," it said.

Harry voted "yes"— and with that, 27 million American women got the constitutional right to vote.

That fall, women across the country went to vote for the first time in American history. The fight had lasted seventy-two years — so long that only one woman from the Seneca Falls Convention was still alive. She was Charlotte Woodward, the young glove maker. When she cast her ballot, she was ninety-one years old.

A Place to Visit
Women's Rights National Historical Park
136 Fall Street, Seneca Falls, NY 13148
315-568-2991   http://www.nps.gov/wori/